"There is a striking a͏[
ative to the time of c
them that is calculated to enhance the quality not only of
prayer, but of its extension into the other activities of the
day. The one who uses these prayers for an extended
time will, I suspect, begin not only to pray better but to
feel more alive and more fully present to God throughout the day."

Abbot John E. Bamberger
Abbey of the Genesee

"Prayers of the Hours: Morning, Midday and Evening puts
into words so many of the deep desires and longings of
human hearts today. The prayers are fresh and relevant.
This prayer book will make a wonderful resource for
both corporate and private devotion, helping to establish
a rhythm to daily life. The disciplined prayer life of the
author shines through every prayer. Other ministers
could learn from him."

E. Glenn Hinson
Baptist Theological Seminary

"Ideal for family prayers, this book is, like the book of
psalms, very much in touch with the human condition:
our need for God and the blessings and obstacles we
meet on our way to the divine presence. It could well be
called a book of psalms for contemporary people.

"The prayers are strong, vivid, challenging, comfort-
ing, continually returning to basic themes, but each time
with a freshness and originality. Joy, presence, awareness, love and commitment pervade them."

William H. Shannon
General Editor, Thomas Merton Letters

"Pastor Lahman has set before us a series of exercises in the art of learning to pray, exercises that should be helpful to many in developing a meaningful prayer life.

"As one reads these prayers through, one gets a view of the onward progression of God's time or, perhaps, our progression through God's time. I predict that this little devotional handbook will become meaningful to many and the companion to many more."

Michael Ogden, M.D.
Psychiatrist

"*Prayers of the Hours* is a heart to heart talk with our loving Creator. Sensitive to the rhythms of our life, James Lahman begins with the basic rhythm of each day and skillfully weaves into his prayers our longing for union, peace, justice, and love. This sensitively and beautifully written book is a wonderful gift to all who wish to express their longings in new and creative ways."

Sr. Agnes Otting
Waldbreitbach, Germany

"James Lahman offers a gift of daily prayers, which combine the freshness of one person's struggles in faith with language drawn from the Bible and the tradition. There is here an earnestness about the discipline of prayer, but more important the affirmation that prayer is conversation with the God who surrounds us with grace and mercy. Above all, there is a witness to the fact that every moment of the day is lived in the presence of God and that presence is always greater than anything that we can do or say."

Peter Schmiechen
President, Lancaster Theological Seminary

PRAYERS
OF THE HOURS
MORNING MIDDAY & EVENING

JAMES RICHARD LAHMAN

TWENTY-THIRD PUBLICATIONS
Mystic, Connecticut 06355

Twenty-Third Publications
185 Willow Street
P.O. Box 180
Mystic, CT 06355
(203) 536-2611
800-321-0411

ISBN 0-89622-677-8
Library of Congress Catalog Card Number 95-61503
Printed in the U.S.A.

Contents

Introduction

Written private prayers are not unlike a personal diary. One puts one's innermost self in it. They are also like a private journal—a record and a clarification of one's most private thoughts in relationship to God. Private prayers are an individual's "Kyrie Eleison" and "Sanctus" all bound up in one.

It was the custom of Jesus and also of his faith community to pray three times each day—morning, midday, and evening. He also prayed at meal time. But prayer for him was more than merely praying at "set" times; it represented a continual and constant state of being at one with God. Prayer for Jesus was intimacy with God.

Prayer is divine-human intimacy. Prayer is not merely talking to God; at its deepest level it involves a "listening." Prayer is listening to God. Being quiet. Shutting out the exterior noise and the busyness of modern living. Gaining

1

possession of one's inner life. Prayer is the culti-
vation of an authentic interior life. God initiates,
welcomes, and provides hospitality for divine-
human intimacy. Authentic prayer is to have
one's heart and mind unclouded and oriented
toward God.

If one learns to pray by praying, one learns
about oneself by praying. The praying individual is compelled to ask and to answer several
basic questions about self and God. To whom is
one directing one's prayers? What is the nature
of the God to whom one is praying? What are
the appropriate adjectives for addressing God?
Are there any appropriate pronouns with which
one can rightly refer to God?

This little volume is not an essay on the the-
ology of prayer, nor is it an explanation of one
or another theory of prayer. Rather it is a collec-
tion of morning, midday, and evening prayers.
There are such prayers for each day of the
month with a biblical passage (a long and a
short form) for reflection at day's end.

This offering of private daily prayers is
intended as a springboard to enable the reader
to develop his or her own daily prayers—and
the habit of prayer.

"More tears are shed over answered prayers
than unanswered ones."

Teresa of Avila

"…the only way to pray is to pray; and the way
to pray well is to pray much."

Dom John Chapman

"We must pray not first of all because it feels
good or helps, but because God loves us and
wants our attention."

Henri J. M. Nouwen

Day 1

Morning

Caring God who watches over, nourishes, and invites me into union, as I begin this new day I offer thanks for the sleep, the rest, and the restorative gifts to my body and mind. Holy God, you have watched over me while I did not know it. You have awakened me with wholeness of body and spirit. As you have blessed me in the silent watches of the night, enable me to make of this new day a gift to you. Visit my energies, skills, and talents with a touch of divine grace so that when night comes I may present my gift with joy and thanksgiving. Great Companion of all people, Holy Spirit, Truth Divine, to you I pray. Amen.

Midday

Most Holy God, great and magnificent Liberator, this day is half over and already your gift of time has been consumed by things of little or no significance. Well-meaning intentions, good planning, and sharp focus give way to interruptions. Minor irritations become the objects of hidden blessings. You who are beyond yet within busyness, help me to know, see, and receive grace even in the midst of the routine and the ordinary. Enable me to use these afternoon hours in ways so that my life exhibits noble intentions. Most intimate spiritual Companion and Friend, bless my use of time. In the Name of Christ Jesus, I pray. Amen.

Evening

At day's end I pause before I sleep and gather the fragments of all that I have and have not been this day. For blessings that came as surprises and nourished my very being; for blessings received and gone unnoticed, forgive. During all of the watches of the night, grant my body and mind peaceful sleep and rest. Watch over my family in all of its various components and over all those who are precious to me. May the night's rest bring new insight and strength for my being a creative instrument of Christ's healing love and wholeness. To the great Physician and Good Shepherd, I pray in trust, believing. Amen.

Scripture

O God, you are my God, I seek you, my soul thirsts for you; my flesh faints for you, as in a dry and weary land where there is no water.

So I have looked upon you in the sanctuary, beholding your power and glory. Because your steadfast love is better than life, my lips will praise you. So I will bless you as long as I live; I will lift up my hands and call on your name.

Psalm 63:1–4

.... my soul thirsts for you....

Psalm 63:2

7

Day 2

Morning

Intervening, all-embracing, triune God, with the first sounds of morning you awaken me and my mind becomes conscious that I am again alive. By your merciful grace, my sensitivities are awakened to the newness of joys and possibilities that await my discovery. As you have watched over me while I slept, and have kept my mind and body free from harm's way; through these awakening hours be my constant companion and guide, thus enabling me to be fully alive. Infuse all of my life with your Holy Spirit, to the sole end and purpose that I may be this day a voice and a presence of your holy healing, hope, and caring. Amen.

Midday

Wonderful God of wholeness and peace, you know all. You invite decency, welcome honesty, encourage integrity, embrace purity; and you neither cast out nor abandon any. Since the breaking of dawn you have been near me. You have blessed me, and I have been oblivious. Teach me how to more readily recognize your presence. Now, at this midday I pause to gain perspective, refocus, and gather new energy. Enable me in these unused hours to penetrate the puzzle of language. Empower me to see inside its mystery and to employ language, as do the Psalmist and the poet. May these moments of quietness draw me closer to you; and may I be a more fruitful instrument of your Divine Peace. Amen.

Evening

Amazing God who is always present, in the very beginning, at the dawn of creation, you separated the light from darkness creating both night and day; a time for both rest and work. Now that the evening shadows have brought to a close the work of this day, enable me to rest. Set me free from the stress and strain of work. For any errors in judgment that I may have made, for any slight of friend or stranger, for any acts of mercy that called out and went unheeded, for any sign of grace that went unnoticed, for anything left undone, and for anything done that was less than holy, dear God, forgive. Watch over me while I sleep, and grant me peace and restorative rest. Wake me at dawn with newness of life. Amen.

Scripture

For God alone my soul waits in silence, for my hope is from him. He alone is my rock and my salvation, my fortress; I shall not be shaken. On God rests my deliverance and my honor; my mighty rock, my refuge is in God. Trust in him at all times, O people; pour out your heart before him; God is a refuge for us.

Psalm 62:6–9

For God alone my soul waits in silence, for my hope is from him.

Psalm 62:6

Day 3

Morning

Generous God of mercy, peace, and wholeness, who invites all of creation into union, you have blessed me while I slept, and I knew it not. In the hours of sleep you gifted me with refreshing rest, and you restored my body and mind to newness. Enable me to know, see, and feel this new day as a gift given in trust. Through these awakening hours be my constant companion and soul guide. Sharpen my reasoning, broaden my thinking, and stand my sensitivities at attention; that I may live this day fully alive and in an intentional manner. By the Holy Cross of Jesus, I pray. Amen.

Midday

Merciful and mighty God of ultimates and intimacy, tenderhearted is your Holy Spirit. You encompass all that is. Your outstretched arms embrace all; you invite me to come closer. You encourage me to use both my heart and mind in grasping the Divine Mystery. At midday I pause to recollect memories of forgotten blessings. May these brief moments of reflection bring new insight. Help me to keep body and soul together, and to know the unity of the Holy Trinity. May the unused hours of my life this day be useful in your sight. Empower me in faithfulness. Amen.

Evening

Now that the evening shadows have fallen on this day and my work has been completed, I seek to put aside all of those unfinished tasks and to rest. Unclutter my mind of useless chatter, and grant me fruitful silence. Let there be parity of rest and work in my life, and help me to actively seek a wholesome balance. Almighty, eternal, and nurturing God, for each of those discernable moments of your Presence this day I am thankful, and ask forgiveness for all of those times I was oblivious. Grant my body healing rest, restore my spirit, renew my energies; and while I sleep, grant me peace. In the Holy Name of Christ Jesus, I make this prayer. Amen.

Scripture

Bless the LORD, O my soul, and all that is within me, bless his holy name. Bless the LORD, O my soul, and do not forget all his benefits—who forgives all your iniquity, who heals all your diseases, who redeems your life from the Pit, who crowns you with steadfast love and mercy, who satisfies you with good as long as you live so that your youth is renewed like the eagle's.

Psalm 103:1–5

Bless the LORD, O my soul, and all that is within me, bless his holy name.

Psalm 103:1

Day 4

Morning

Amazing God who never grows weary in the care and cure of my soul, daily you pull me toward wholeness, and you continuously invite me into union. In each hour of this day, bless me with the awareness that your Presence dwells with all that is human. Enable my eyes to see, my mind to know, my heart to feel, that even in the life of the lowliest and most broken, your indwelling Presence is. Help me to recognize you, and to affirm your Holy Presence by my actions with all whom I encounter this day. In the name of the Triune God, Father, Son, and Holy Spirit, I pray. Amen.

Midday

In the midst of the heat and rush of this summer day, at midday I pause momentarily to think about the source and final purpose of my life. Great Creator and ever-creating God; mighty-loving God of mercy, justice, and peace; wonderful-caring and advocating God for my full humanity and liberation, you invite, welcome, and encourage me to spend time just being quiet. Although the heat is oppressive, it is a forceful call to being, which is more powerful than doing. Amazing God for whom I labor, even the summer heat beckons me to seek you. Under the shadow of the Cross of Christ, I come to pray. Amen.

Evening

entle God of peace and compassion, day is over and night has come. Help me now to place in your hands all that this day has been. Into your eternal care I release all of the anxieties, frustrations, and cares that I have known this day. Set me free from every burden that the day has brought, and grant me restorative rest. While I wait for sleep, I count the blessings received and noticed since I woke. I pray in the Holy Name of Christ Jesus, my Redeemer and Friend. Amen.

Scripture

I will extol you, O Lord, for you have drawn me up, and did not let my foes rejoice over me. O Lord my God, I cried to you for help, and you have healed me. O Lord, you brought up my soul from Sheol, restored me to life from among those gone down to the Pit.

You have turned my mourning into dancing; you have taken off my sackcloth and clothed me with joy, so that my soul may praise you and not be silent. O Lord my God, I will give thanks to you forever.

Psalm 30:2–4; 12–13

O Lord my God, I cried to you for help, and you have healed me.

Psalm 30:3

Day 5

Morning

Holy Spirit, truth divine, on all of the paths that I tread this day, be my most intimate companion, and be close by my side each hour. Let no dullness of mind, or any preoccupation with the immediate, or any pressing concern with the urgent, pull me away and sever the tether that is life-giving. Help me to be alert and watchful for the unfolding of this day's gifts of wonder, surprise, and mystery. By the recognition of these new gifts bless my mind, my heart, and my soul. In the Name of the Triune God, I pray. Amen.

Midday

God, whom I see in the faces of little children; God of innocence and trust; God of honesty and integrity; God who births the best in me and who desires the best for me, at midday I pause for perspective. Enable me to consider the blessings that have passed my way this morning. For friends who are constant and loyal; for the visit of good health; for freedom from anxiety, confusion, and pain; for a mind that can think and reason; for a heart that can feel and lift life and celebrate it. As I gather these remembered blessings, I am refreshed. Empower me with courage to walk by your side; and should I go down some wayward path, call my name and pull me back so that I may continue this life by your side. In the Name of Christ Jesus, I pray. Amen.

Evening

Eternal and mighty God of all,
merciful God of peace, faithful friend
of all who seek you, and most
intimate companion of my soul, during the
daylight hours you visited my life, gifted me,
and blessed me. I am humbled by the volume of
human brokenness, pain, and darkness that I
encounter. Enable my every thought, word, and
act to reveal the healing-saving love of Christ
Jesus. Make and keep whole my body and soul.
Lord Jesus Christ, hold me this night as in the
hollow of your hand. Amen.

Scripture

Hear a just cause, O LORD; attend to my cry; give ear to my prayer from lips free of deceit.

My steps have held fast to your paths; my feet have not slipped. I call upon you, for you will answer me, O God; incline your ear to me, hear my words. Wondrously show your steadfast love, O savior of those who seek refuge from their adversaries at your right hand. Guard me as the apple of the eye; hide me in the shadow of your wings.

Psalm 17:1; 5–8

Guard me as the apple of the eye; hide me in the shadow of your wings.

Psalm 17:8

Day 6

Morning

All-embracing and most caring God, with the gentle sounds of nature you awaken me to the gifts of a new day. My body is tired and slow to respond, but my spirit is fully energized by the possibilities that the new day offers. But already my mind is being bombarded by the sights and sounds of city living: buildings that dwarf tall trees, loud blowing horns, and rushing automobiles that carry hurried-anxious people. Save me, O God, from the speed and the noise that seek to infect my body and soul. Give me an eye to watch for and to see the wonders of your creation—to add to and not destroy; to build up and to nurture; to bless, heal, and to be a joy bringer. In the Blessed Name of Christ Jesus, I pray. Amen.

Midday

Nurturing God of peace, and faithful companion through life's journey, keep me close by your side for the remaining hours of this day. Help me to see the large dimensions of the Gospel of Christ. Help me to articulate with clarity, and to demonstrate with vigor what I feel and know to be true of the Gospel. Help me to use my mind in ways that will enable others to see and know the healing and life-giving reality of the Gospel. May all that I am and all that I have this day, be my gift to you. In the Name of Christ Jesus, I pray. Amen.

Evening

Now that the day is over and my work is done, I ask for your benediction on both my day and deeds. Aid me as I prepare for sleep to recollect each one of those points of grace when, where, and how I have been blessed. Let me not trivialize any one of those gifts. Truly your blessings on my life are as numerous as the stars and the sand. Help me to recall all of them, and to live in memory of these gifts. Teach me the content of prayer, and may my life reflect my prayers. I gently hold the Bethlehem baby, and pray. Amen.

Scripture

How lovely is your dwelling place, O LORD of hosts! My soul longs, indeed it faints for the courts of the LORD; my heart and my flesh sing for joy to the living God. Even the sparrow finds a home, and the swallow a nest for herself, where she may lay her young, at your altars, O LORD of hosts, my King and my God. Happy are those who live in your house, ever singing your praise.

For a day in your courts is better than a thousand elsewhere. I would rather be a doorkeeper in the house of my God than live in the tents of wickedness.

Psalm 84:1–5; 11

Even the sparrow finds a home, and the swallow a nest for herself....

Psalm 84:4

Day 7

Morning

Tender-hearted God of mercy, you continue to care for me even while I knowingly evade the presence of holiness. Within and beyond the clamoring noises of the workplace, help me this day to be conscious of your freely given grace, and of your continuous invitation and welcome into deeper realms of holiness. Enable me to live each hour of this day in such a manner that your life-giving gifts will not be lost on me. Bless my living in ways that will be a blessing to others. In the Holy Name of Jesus, I pray. Amen.

Midday

Amazing God of hope, faith, and courage, at midday help me to place aside all momentary concerns, to pull back the blinders, and to look within. Barefoot and with bowed head, leaving all fears and anxieties behind, I seek to draw near to that realm of holiness which is beyond thoughts and words. In these moments of silence do some mighty work in the depths of my soul. Keep me on my knees until my heart is strong and courageous. Strengthen my mind by the indwelling of the Holy Spirit. Mighty God of mercy, use all of me; heart, mind, body, and soul for your liberating work of peace and justice. By the power of your grace I believe, and pray. Amen.

Evening

Amazing, eternal, almighty, gentle, merciful, and most intimate God, the evening shadows have brought to a close this day. I have endeavored to be faithful with the hours entrusted to me. Enable me in these early evening hours to give back to you all of my deeds and dreams of this day. Grant me a clear conscience, a true heart, and a soul that is pure. Grant me this night restful sleep and fresh dreams that will empower, embolden, and ennoble me for the new day. Use all of my heart, mind, body, and soul for your Holiness. By the side of the new mother, Mary, I look into the eyes of the Bethlehem baby and, like him in innocence and need, I pray. Amen.

Scripture

You who live in the shelter of the Most High, who abide in the shadow of the Almighty, will say to the LORD, "My refuge and my fortress; my God, in whom I trust." For he will deliver you from the snare of the fowler and from the deadly pestilence; he will cover you with his pinions, and under his wings you will find refuge; his faithfulness is a shield and buckler. You will not fear the terror of the night, or the arrow that flies by day, or the pestilence that stalks in darkness, or the destruction that wastes at noonday.

Psalm 91:1–6

...under his wings you will find refuge....

Psalm 91:4

Day 8

Morning

Great, eternal, most gentle and still creating God, at this early morning hour you have already visited my life—there is surprise and joy. My mind and my heart are being called to attention. Help me to use this early morning Epiphany in each of the several paths that I tread this day. May the Holy Spirit be my constant companion and help me to view my life in the light of your ongoing creation. Wipe the dimness from my eyes that I may see. Fill each of the hollow spaces in my heart with a spirit of holy feeling and thinking. By the cross of Jesus my Redeemer, I pray. Amen.

Midday

Your Holy Spirit calls out to me, calling me to quiet and reflection. Before I can remember my need or my desire to pray, you call me to my better self. Now at midday, I pause to recollect all that this day has offered to me, and my limited response to that sacred gift. It is with a spirit of humility and of shame that I enter, intimately, into your Presence. Deliver me from the rush and the noise around me, and set me free from all such forces that would occupy my life and hold me captive. Take my mind and use it in new and creative ways to bring healing and hope to others. In the Name of Christ Jesus, I pray. Amen.

Evening

Almighty and amazing God, now that day is over and my work is done, receive all of my dreams and deeds into your care. In these evening hours grant me quiet and peace. Before I sleep, let me reflect on this day's Epiphany. Empower me with the perception to recognize the extraordinary nature of ordinary blessings: for heart and hand, for eye and ear, for arm and leg, for taste and touch, for speech and sound; and for the gifts of thinking, feeling, and reasoning. In the presence of such extraordinary gifts my life stands at attention. Teach me how to use all that I am for your holiness. With the Wise Men I bring my gift, kneel, and pray. Amen.

Scripture

O give thanks to the LORD, for he is good; for his steadfast love endures forever. Let the redeemed of the LORD say so, those he redeemed from trouble.... Some wandered in desert wastes, finding no way to an inhabited town; hungry and thirsty, their soul fainted within them. Then they cried to the LORD in their trouble, and he delivered them from their distress; he led them by a straight way, until they reached an inhabited town. Let them thank the LORD for his steadfast love, for his wonderful works to humankind. For he satisfies the thirsty, and the hungry he fills with good things.

Psalm 107:1–2; 4–9

Let the redeemed of the LORD say so....

Psalm 107:2

Day 9

Morning

Mighty, caring, and nourishing God, grace my life with the inner resolve, that this day all of my thoughts, energies, and desires will be focused solely on your divine purposes. Enabling God, help me to bring sharper focus to the central nature of my life's work. Empower me by your grace to deploy my mind, body, and soul as a living energy for the cause of Christ. In the Holy Name of Jesus, my Redeemer and strength, I pray. Amen.

Midday

Merciful and mighty God, you gift me daily with blessings beyond imagining and deserving. Sometimes I am alert to those grace-filled gifts; other times I am preoccupied with lesser concerns and am oblivious both to your presence and to the gifts in front of me waiting to be received. Empowering-nurturing God, forgive my callousness, and once again draw me closer to your Presence. During the remaining hours of this day, grant me your own strength and discernment; equip me with your powers of healing and blessing. Keep me faithful to the Gospel and to Christ, in whose Holy Name, I pray. Amen.

Evening

Almighty God of every living thing and of all that is yet to be, in your presence my life is transparent. You surround my life with blessings more numerous than I can count. Help me to rise out of my affluence all the way up to the level of poverty that Jesus knew. Help me to see and know the ordinary and regular things of life as gifts and blessings. Help me to freely share the gifts of my heart and mind; and may all of my possessions be at your constant and immediate disposal. As you have blessed my day, now bless my sleep with rest and my dreams with insight. In the name of hope, peace, and love, I pray. Amen.

Scripture

I lift up my eyes to the hills—from where will my help come? My help comes from the LORD, who made heaven and earth. He will not let your foot be moved; he who keeps you will not slumber. He who keeps Israel will neither slumber nor sleep. The LORD is your keeper; the LORD is your shade at your right hand. The sun shall not strike you by day, nor the moon by night. The LORD will keep you from all evil; he will keep your life. The LORD will keep your going out and your coming in from this time on and forevermore.

Psalm 121

The LORD is your keeper; the LORD is your shade at your right hand.

Psalm 121:5

Day 10

Morning

You who are guardian, companion, and lover of my eternal soul, help me this day to be watchful for and observant of the visitation of your holy angels. You invite me into union, but never coerce. Frequently I am preoccupied with the immediate, overly busy with urgent things, and oblivious to your inviting, nourishing Presence. At the beginning of this new day grace every cell of my mind, body, and soul with your calming, whole-making peace. Enable me through each awakening hour to be your faithful servant and true witness. In the Name of Christ, who sets me free and gives me strength, I pray. Amen.

Midday

Powerful-gentle God of every comfort and good hope, amid the rush of a hectic schedule, at midday, you call me to prayer. Your all-embracing Presence calls me to transcend the present moment and to see the light and fullness of eternity. As I recount your Presence at the various critical junctures in my life, I am both humbled and thankful. From my birth, you have watched over, nurtured, protected, and blessed me. This day, you have blessed me with the uncommon gifts of health and wholeness. You gift me with faith, and teach me the secrets of viewing and keeping body and soul together. Lead me on, mighty God, through this day. In the name of the Holy Spirit, my Guardian, I pray. Amen.

Evening

Most intimate God of everything that ever was, is, or shall yet be, you know my most secret thoughts. You know my aspirations and my dreams. You know everything about me. Still you bless, comfort, forgive, restore, and renew my life day after day. Day is over and work is done; grant me rest, sleep, and peace. Enable me to come closer to your holiness. Empower me to become that which you will me to be. Under the shadow of the Cross of Jesus, I pray. Amen.

Scripture

O LORD, you have searched me and known me. You know when I sit down and when I rise up; you discern my thoughts from far away. You search out my path and my lying down, and are acquainted with all my ways. Even before a word is on my tongue, O LORD, you know it completely. You hem me in, behind and before, and lay your hand upon me. Such knowledge is too wonderful for me; it is so high that I cannot attain it.

Psalm 139:1–6

Such knowledge is too wonderful for me; it is so high that I cannot attain it.

Psalm 139:6

Day 11

Morning

Almighty God of creation and eternity, within your providence we live and our lives discover their meaning. Enable me this day to see some glimpse of the grandeur of your creation. In the midst of the holiness around me, help me to walk and to speak with an awareness that all that is human is of your creation and thus Holy. At the beginning of this new day, grace my total being, alert my sensitivities that I may see, hear, and feel the minute details of your creation. Empower me to see all that is human as the crowning achievement of creation, capable of blessing and also in need of it. Through the hours of this day, walk with me in each of my several paths. In the Name of Christ, my Holy Friend, and my Redeemer, I pray. Amen.

Midday

God of every comfort and good hope, I am thankful that at midday I can pause from my labors, be momentarily quiet, and listen for your calling upon me to be my higher-deeper self. Mighty merciful God, equip me with new skills and powers of discernment; help me see and to know with clarity, where and how your healing and holiness can be provided to those who need miracles in their lives. Teach me how to be your Ambassador of hope, holiness, and healing. Enable me with new understanding and freshness to "point the way" and to introduce the One who delivers miracles. In the Holy Name of Christ, I pray, believing. Amen.

Evening

Great and wonderful God of justice and hope, you reveal yourself in great and small ways. Your holiness invites the lowliest of your servants into your Presence. Before you my life is transparent. Let there be in me no false humility, nor vain pride. Holy God, your merciful companionship knows no limits. As I lay my body down to sleep, enable me to also lay down the frustrations, the stresses, and all of the anxieties of this day. As you have blessed my work, bless my sleep. In the watches of the night heal all of me: heart, mind, body, and soul. Awaken me with the dawn that I may pray before I work. Amen.

Scripture

Where can I go from your spirit? Or where can I flee from your presence? If I ascend to heaven, you are there; if I make my bed in Sheol, you are there. If I take the wings of the morning and settle at the farthest limits of the sea, even there your hand shall lead me, and your right hand shall hold me fast. If I say, "Surely the darkness shall cover me, and the light around me become night," even the darkness is not dark to you; the night is as bright as the day, for darkness is as light to you.

Psalm 139:7–12

...even the darkness is not dark to you....

Psalm 139:12

Day 12

Morning

God of abundant mercy and endless supply of surprises, you who are faithful beyond our imagining and more loving than our deserving, grace my life again with your Peace and your very own Presence. Bless all of my thoughts, desires, actions, and energies and direct them in ways that birth and foster in others wholesomeness and healing. Walk with me this day and keep my soul whole and free of sin. In the Name of Christ, my Redeemer and Holy Friend, I pray. Amen.

Midday

All-embracing, gentle God of peace and good will, help me to be intentional and to carefully name the adjectives that I ascribe to your Holiness. In my midday prayers move me beyond thanksgiving that is trivial and confession that is trite. Make your dwelling place in my innermost consciousness. Move me at the depths of my being. Awaken me with the felt knowledge of your indwelling Presence, and enable me to have the "senses" to know, to welcome, and to provide hospitality to your Holiness. Within the outstretched arms of the crucified Lord, I pray. Amen.

Evening

Merciful, mighty God of heights and depths, and of all that is in between, you invite me to come into the circle of your all-seeing, all-knowing, and all-embracing presence. Within the circle of your Holiness, all that I am is transparent. I stand like Adam and Eve in the garden, like Moses before the burning bush, like the child Samuel in the middle of the night, like Elijah recognizing the still small voice, and like the young Mary hearing the voice of an angel. Keep me near the circle of your Holiness, and daily nourish my life. By my living, may the vision of your Holiness deepen in me. In the Name of Christ Jesus, I pray. Amen.

Scripture

ow weighty to me are your thoughts, O God! How vast is the sum of them! I try to count them—they are more than the sand; I come to the end—I am still with you.

Search me, O God, and know my heart; test me and know my thoughts. See if there is any wicked way in me, and lead me in the way everlasting.

Psalm 139:17–18; 23–24

How weighty to me are your thoughts....

Psalm 139:17

Day 13

Morning

Great caring God, you love, bless, and care for each one, as if we were the only ones in your repertoire in need. You love me, care for me, watch over me, like my own mother. You prod and provoke me into betterness. Awaken within me new vistas of love, gentleness, and tenderheartedness. With your own creative Presence surround all the dark, secret corners of my life, fill me with purity of heart and wholesomeness of act. You know all about me, have faith in me, and will the best for me. Dwell within my soul this day. By his side, and in the outstretched arms of the Mother of Jesus, I pray. Amen.

Midday

Great divine mystery, with perfect motherly care, you gift me with freedom that is unrestricted and you trust my humanity. Freely and willingly you give of yourself to me. You are never far away. When I am in pain and suffering, emotionally or physically, you are near. You grace my life with all things needful. You welcome me into divine intimacy. You encourage me to live a holy view of humanity. Put truth into my prayers and enable me to so live. Walk with me, lest I walk alone and stumble. In the Holy Name of Christ Jesus, my Redeemer, I pray. Amen.

Evening

Wonderful, amazing, ever-present God, your mercies and blessings are always fresh and in abundance. Teach my heart to feel as the heart of Jesus felt. Help me to be thankful more quickly. Train my eye to recognize more readily the regular miracles that daily visit. Tune my mind to affirm that your mercies and judgments are at work all over this world, and that you cannot be contained, harnessed, or evaded. Great lover of my soul, protect and nourish me throughout this night and awaken me to the gift of a new day. In the Holy Name of Christ Jesus, my Redeemer, I pray. Amen.

Scripture

ear my prayer, O LORD; give ear to my supplications in your faithfulness; answer me in your righteousness. Do not enter into judgment with your servant, for no one living is righteous before you.

I remember the days of old, I think about all your deeds, I meditate on the works of your hands. I stretch out my hands to you; my soul thirsts for you like a parched land. Answer me quickly, O LORD; my spirit fails. Do not hide your face from me, or I shall be like those who go down to the Pit. Let me hear of your steadfast love in the morning, for in you I put my trust. Teach me the way I should go, for to you I lift up my soul.

Psalm 143:1–2; 5–8

Let me hear of your steadfast love in the morning, for in you I put my trust.

Psalm 143:8

Day 14

Morning

Amazing God of surprise visits, gift me with awakened sensitivities that can feel, see, and know your Presence. Deepen me down until my heart and mind utter the knowledge that resides in my soul. Set me free from all forms of human bondage and everything else that enslaves my being. Lift my life this day, my spirit, my heart, and my mind, until I am in true alignment with the fullness of your holy will. Engrave on my heart and mind the knowledge that lives eternally in my soul. Under the shadow of the Cross and by the side of Peter, Thomas, and James, I stand in silence and pray. Amen.

Midday

Merciful and mighty God of compassion and watchful care, now, at midday, strengthen again my life with mercy and peace. Help me to pause and to reflect on the essence, the substance, and the ultimates of my living. Empower me to discern what is transitory and what is essential and life-enhancing. Help me to bring your healing Presence wherever there is pain or brokenness; help me to provide clarity of thought wherever there is confusion and misunderstanding; help me to be your ambassador wherever there is mistrust and anger; and help me to be an exemplary representative of the Gospel to those who know not of your liberating-redeeming Presence. In all things and in all ways, empower me to be a faithful example of the living Christ alive within me. Amen.

Evening

Wonderful-amazing God, your nurturing Presence is constant and continual, and when I become oblivious to your nearness, you reveal yourself in grace-filled moments, places, and means, that both surprise and call my soul back to attention. Help me to learn the skills of recollection that I may remember and recall all of your special visitations to my life. May my mind be ever alert, my heart ever receptive, and my eyes see your Presence at work in the lives of others. Teach me about the art of healing that I may learn to be a healer. Amen.

Scripture

I will extol you, my God and King, and
bless your name forever and ever. Every
day I will bless you, and praise your
name forever and ever. Great is the LORD, and
greatly to be praised; his greatness is unsearchable.

On the glorious splendor of your majesty,
and on your wondrous works, I will meditate.
The might of your awesome deeds shall be pro-
claimed, and I will declare your greatness.

The LORD is gracious and merciful, slow to
anger and abounding in steadfast love. The
LORD is good to all, and his compassion is over
all that he has made.

Psalm 145:1–3; 5–6; 8–9

On the glorious splendor of your majesty, and
on your wondrous works, I will meditate.

Psalm 145:5

Day 15

Morning

God of all mystery, blessings, and holy surprises, at the beginning of this new day I pause to remember how often and for how long you have involved yourself in my life. Grace my life this hour with a fuller recollection. Deliver me from my own self-imposed isolation, but save me from the speed and noise of these times. Lift up my heart, my soul, and my mind to see purity and innocence. Walk by my side until dreams become deeds. Help me to remember who I belong to and why I am. In the Name of Christ, my faithful Friend and Redeemer, I pray. Amen.

Midday

ighty God of every good comfort, you watch over me as if You had no other creature with whom to occupy your attention. You care for, protect, nurture, and gift me with blessings daily. You awaken me from my slumber, my occasional drifting, and nudge me on the path of faithfulness. You encourage me to examine and define my being in the light of the living Christ—my companion and guardian. You have given me a heart that is well and a mind that can be alert. You ask only that I, in service to others, make full use of heart, mind, and soul. As examples of both faith and sin, I claim as brothers: Peter, James, Andrew, and Thomas. In the Garden with Mary, I pray. Amen.

Evening

God of all majesty, mystery, and mercy, your Holiness surrounds and permeates all that I am. From you nothing is concealed. Your divine nature embraces all and brings newness of life and health. It is your divine will to gift and care for all. You nourish, protect, guide, and befriend me. You invite me to come deeper into your Holiness, and you point me in the direction of larger-wider ways of seeing, acting, and knowing. Now that day is over and my work is finished, grant my mind and body peace and restorative sleep. By the sides of Thomas, Andrew, Nicodemus, and Martha, I kneel and pray. Amen.

Scripture

There the angel of the LORD appeared to Moses in a flame of fire out of a bush; he looked, and the bush was blazing, yet it was not consumed. Then Moses said, "I must turn aside and look at this great sight, and see why the bush is not burned up." When the LORD saw that he had turned aside to see, God called to him out of the bush, "Moses, Moses!" And he said, "Here I am." Then he said, "Come no closer! Remove the sandals from your feet, for the place on which you are standing is holy ground." He said further, "I am the God of your father, the God of Abraham, the God of Isaac, and the God of Jacob." And Moses hid his face, for he was afraid to look at God.

Exodus 3:2–6

Then Moses said, "I must turn aside and look at this great sight, and see why the bush is not burned up."

Exodus 3:3

Day 16

Morning

Almighty, ever-present, caring, and loving beyond my imagining—amazing God, you are always seeking, inviting, and encouraging me to come into closer-deeper divine intimacy. What I seek I am afraid of—except on my own terms. Set me free from all fear. With your beckoning whispers, guide my soul as I come barefoot and with bowed head into the depths of divine union. Lift up my life, heart, mind, body, and soul until my total being becomes a living temple unto you. Within the caring arms of the Mother of Jesus, and under the shadow of his Cross, I pray. Amen.

Midday

Mighty God of everything and everyone, in every place and in every time, the bonds of space, time, and knowledge cannot constrict, contain, or analyze the heights and depths of your amazing grace bestowed unmerited on my life. Great divine mystery, you are "beyond and more than," yet you are as close as a heartbeat. You reach out and invite me to come closer within your embrace of wholeness. Teach me more about silence. Gift me with the virtue of quietness. Empower me with the gift of discernment that is Holy. Continue to strengthen my body and mind until all that I am is wholly yours. Keep me within the circle of all who live, work, and pray for mercy and peace. Amen.

Evening

Mighty God of everything that is and all that is yet to be, prior to my birth you established in my life the innate need for companionship with you. At every present moment you invite and encourage me to come deeper into the realms of Holiness. In my silence, your Holy silence is as thunder. As I bow my head in reverence, teach me also to bow my mind and heart. Sharpen all of my sensitivities; deepen my inner resolve; fill, dwell, and possess all of my unconsciousness until my awakened self is a true reflection of your Holiness. Help me to put honesty in my prayers, and may my living be a faithful reflection of my prayers. In all of my work and play, may your grace bless and make me whole. Amen.

Scripture

Now Samuel did not yet know the LORD, and the word of the LORD had not yet been revealed to him. The LORD called Samuel again, a third time. And he got up and went to Eli, and said, "Here I am, for you called me." Then Eli perceived that the LORD was calling the boy. Therefore Eli said to Samuel, "Go, lie down; and if he calls you, you shall say, 'Speak, LORD, for your servant is listening.'" So Samuel went and lay down in his place.

I Samuel 3:7–9

And Samuel said, "Speak, for your servant is listening."

I Samuel 3:10

Day 17

Morning

Almighty God of miracles yet to be, you believe in me, and will the best in me and for me. This day, empower me to see and to view my life as a gift, a gift given in trust from you. Take my eyes and enable them to see and recognize innocence and purity. Take my heart and enable it to feel some individual's pain. Take my hands and use them in creative ways in lifting someone's burden. Take my mind and use all of it for your glory. Help me this day to use all of my life as a Sacrament. I pray in the Name of Christ Jesus, my Holy friend, companion, and soul guide. Amen.

Midday

Wonderful God of peace and calm, our cultural mores hang heavy over us and exact a large toll from us. We feel pressured by society, peers, and self for more: to desire more, to be more, to achieve more, to accomplish more, and to have more and greater successes. In the midst of running and rushing to catch up and to keep up, we find that (as a society, as a church, and as individuals) speed brings us only more demons. At midday, grant me some moments of quiet and restful repose. On bended knees, I look up to the downcast eyes of the crucified Lord, and I am helped. Amen.

Evening

reat-powerful God of mercy and peace, in your Holy Presence and within your watchful care I daily live. From you no secrets are hidden—or need be! Great lover of my soul, enable me to be an active instrument of your love for and in the world. As you have blessed my life in untold ways, help me to embody your Presence in all of my work and play. In a world of neuroses, violence, and war, empower me to be a peace-giver. May all that I am and all that I seek to do have both your blessing and your judgment. Under the shadow of the Cross I kneel by the side of Thomas, James, and Mary, and pray. Amen.

Scripture

He said, "Go out and stand on the mountain before the LORD, for the LORD is about to pass by." Now there was a great wind, so strong that it was splitting mountains and breaking rocks in pieces before the LORD, but the LORD was not in the wind; and after the wind an earthquake, but the LORD was not in the earthquake; and after the earthquake a fire, but the LORD was not in the fire; and after the fire a sound of sheer silence. When Elijah heard it, he wrapped his face in his mantle and went out and stood at the entrance of the cave. Then there came a voice to him that said, "What are you doing here, Elijah?"

I Kings 19:11–13

....and after the fire a sound of sheer silence.

I Kings 19:12

Day 18

Morning

God of every comfort and good care, you know all: my forgotten sins, my most intimate thoughts, my dreams, my secret desires, and all of my unfulfilled promises. Come and be with me this day. Draw me into your Presence and hold me in your protective-nurturing care until I am stronger and wiser. Within the intimacy of your holy care, nourish my life this day, strengthen my faltering faith, lift my spirit, and feed my soul until I know and recognize innocence and purity as signs of Divine Grace. Enable me to think more clearly, to speak more honestly, to live more courageously, and to believe more powerfully. In the Holy Name of Jesus, I pray. Amen.

Midday

Great caring God of encouragement, comfort, mercy, and peace, we, your human creatures, are needy people. We may be capable of discarding archaic language, yet the experience of the ancient remains ours. We have designed new structures, developed new programs, devised new language; we have even endeavored to "reimagine" the Gospel, and we have discovered that our hearts are indeed restless. Even on my best day I am in need of you. Watch over me in my hour of need. Forgive selfish pride and vain glory. Grant me strength adequate to the tasks that are set in front of me. Flood my life with grace, lest I stumble and fall. In the midst of my work, enable me to discern holiness. Teach me to live tenderheartedness. In faith and joy I kneel by the side of Stephen, Paul, and Barnabas, and pray. Amen.

Evening

God of justice and peace, day is over and night is upon me. This day I have labored for causes and issues that are good. In my work I have had good, sometimes even noble, intentions. At times this day I have been gracious and kind. I have exhibited affection and good will toward others. I have offered thanks for blessings received. I have bowed my head and confessed wrongs. I have been your servant in both word and deed; but I have also rushed in front, trusting in my own perception instead of waiting for the discerning of your Holy Presence. Imprint on my life the discernment that apart from you all is as nothing. Wake me by dawn that I may pray again. In the Spirit of Christ Jesus, I pray. Amen.

Scripture

Then the LORD answered Job out of the whirlwind: "Who is this that darkens counsel by words without knowledge? Gird up your loins like a man, I will question you, and you shall declare to me. Where were you when I laid the foundation of the earth? Tell me, if you have understanding.

"Have you commanded the morning since your days began, and caused the dawn to know its place...?"

Job 38:1–4; 12

Then the LORD answered Job out of the whirlwind....

Job 38:1

Day 19

Morning

Great lover of my soul and faithful daily companion, enable me to be intentionally conscious of your abiding nearness. On each of the various paths that I walk this day, let me not lose sight of your Holy Presence; and if by chance I am distracted by any of the twists or turns, may the memory of this morning prayer call me back to my intentions and to your wholeness. Enable me to provide healing, hope, and wholeness to any that is in need. May my witness be clear, strong, and courageous. May my faith be actualized in my living. Holy Spirit, Truth Divine, to you my prayers are continuous. Amen.

Midday

Gentle God of all creation and of eternity, if there were a "Big Bang" that sent the planets spinning into their orbits, you were there with laughter and majesty. If there shall be something like a "Big Crunch," you likewise will be there. We, your creatures, who live in space and time, contemplate our existence within your providence of holiness, grace, and power. In our spiritual poverty, human arrogance, and sinful pride, supplant the beast within us. Breathe on me again, O Holy Breath, until my whole self exhales loving kindness. This day may the living Christ find in me a welcome abode, and may my living make goodness attractive. At noon, with the felt calmness of Christ on my life, I pray. Amen.

Evening

For blessings of the day that I failed to discern, and for all blessings treated common, forgive. Cleanse my sight that I may see clearly the extraordinary blessings of the regular. For blessings of this day remembered I give thanks, and I am blessed a second time with the power of memory. As you invite me to come closer into the Circle of Holiness, deepen my faith and expand my vision of the ordinary. Make whole my soul. Bless my mind with rest and freshness. In strength and with peace, I pray in the Name of Christ Jesus. Amen.

Scripture

In the year that King Uzziah died, I saw the Lord sitting on a throne, high and lofty; and the hem of his robe filled the temple. Seraphs were in attendance above him; each had six wings: with two they covered their faces, and with two they covered their feet, and with two they flew. And one called to another and said: "Holy, holy, holy is the LORD of hosts; the whole earth is full of his glory." The pivots on the thresholds shook at the voices of those who called, and the house filled with smoke.

Then I heard the voice of the Lord saying, "Whom shall I send, and who will go for us?" And I said, "Here am I; send me!"

Isaiah 6:1–4; 8

Then I heard the voice of the Lord saying, "Whom shall I send, and who will go for us?" And I said, "Here am I; send me!"

Isaiah 6:8

Day 20

Morning

Mighty God of all hope and every comfort, as I start this new day with freshness and freedom from new pressing-urgent concerns, I pause to offer thanks for my parents, teachers, preachers, community leaders, and for friends who have nurtured, sustained, and blessed me on life's way. Burn the power of these life-giving memories into my heart, and may the recalling of these extraordinary blessings by ordinary people help me to pattern my life toward humbleness and thanksgiving. Grow my memory this day, awaken my mind, and strengthen my body toward union with you, my Creator, and my Redeemer. Amen.

Midday

ighty God of All, you have created this wonderful world and all that is. You have placed us, your "highly developed" creatures, in this Garden of Eden. You have gifted us with wisdom and freedom. You have taught us the very essence of life. You have made available for our employ and consumption all things needful. Enable us who have all things to learn the ancient way of sharing, caring, and giving. At midday help me to regain my focus and to spend the remaining hours of this day, fully alive in Eden. Amen.

Evening

Mighty-wonderful God of time and space, of all creatures small and great, you see and know all that is and all that shall yet be. This day has come to its close, the evening shadows have fallen, and work is done. Now as I rest and prepare for sleep, bless these evening hours with quiet and reflection. Take the busyness and the rushing from my life and grant me stillness and calm. As I prepare for sleep, bless my heart, mind, and body with restorative rest. Watch over me during the several watches of the night. May the sounds of dawn awaken me to the newness of your new day. Beneath and within the shadow of the Cross, and with the family of Mary, James, and Thomas, I pray. Amen.

Scripture

On that day, when evening had come, he said to them, "Let us go across to the other side." And leaving the crowd behind, they took him with them in the boat, just as he was. Other boats were with him. A great windstorm arose, and the waves beat into the boat, so that the boat was already being swamped. But he was in the stern, asleep on the cushion; and they woke him up and said to him, "Teacher, do you not care that we are perishing?" He woke up and rebuked the wind, and said to the sea, "Peace! Be still!" Then the wind ceased, and there was a dead calm. He said to them, "Why are you afraid? Have you still no faith?"

Mark 4:35–40

"Have you still no faith?"

Mark 4:40

Day 21

Morning

God of unlimited blessings, your gifts continue to unfold around me and to grace me with an awareness of your nearness. You invite and encourage me to come into the sanctity of divine intimacy. In your Presence of Holiness, you disclose the fullness of my humanity—both its grandeur and its brokenness. Brighten my eyes to see both. Burn into my heart the whole of the Gospel. With awakened joy and gladness of life, embolden me to live what I believe and to believe more fully. In thanksgiving, with joy and praise, I make this morning prayer to my Creator, Redeemer, and Friend. Amen.

Midday

Wonderful God of salvation and health, at midday I pause to think of the things that matter most and get the least attention. For the good green earth that nourishes and gives life and exacts no toll. For the mystery and magnificence of the sun and the moon, and for the plenteous gifts of nature. For birds and bees and falling leaves. For the memory of summer flowers, for the honeysuckle, the hollyhock, and the discovery of a new wildflower. These ordinary gifts stir my spirit and nourish my soul. Aid me with eyes that see and a heart that can feel the intangibles of life, for by such I am being made whole. Amen.

Evening

Merciful, mighty, magnificent, wonderful, faithful companion in all of life's journey, great lover of peace and of my soul, during the hours of this day you have watched over me, blessed me, and breathed on me the very breath of life. Much of the work that I envisaged as part of this day's labor has gone unfinished and must wait another day. For the gifts of this day received and apprehended, I recount and give thanks. Now at the close of day as I take my rest, restore my soul, refresh my mind and body. Watch over and protect me while I sleep. In the Holy Name of Christ Jesus, I pray. Amen.

Scripture

Now the word of the LORD came to me saying, "Before I formed you in the womb I knew you, and before you were born I consecrated you...." Then I said, "...Truly I do not know how to speak, for I am only a boy." But the LORD said to me, "Do not say, 'I am only a boy'; for you shall go to all to whom I send you, and you shall speak whatever I command you. Do not be afraid of them, for I am with you...." Then the LORD put out his hand and touched my mouth; and the LORD said to me, "Now I have put my words in your mouth. See, today I appoint you over nations and over kingdoms, to pluck up and to pull down, to destroy and to overthrow, to build and to plant."

Jeremiah 1:4–10

Then I said, "Ah, Lord God! Truly I do not know how to speak, for I am only a boy."

Jeremiah 1:6

Day 22

Morning

Holy God, merciful Savior, and great Companion of my soul, at the beginning of this new day it is my intention to place all of my skills, talents, and energies at your Divine disposal. May my interior life be filled with innocence and purity, and may all of my activities be a faithful reflection of my interior life. Bless my intentions and deploy all of me as you will. Grant me peace and tranquility, but spare me not a troubled mind or soul wherever, however or whenever you will. I pray in the Holy Name of Christ Jesus, my Redeemer, and my Friend. Amen.

Midday

Merciful God of comfort and hope, at midday you call my heart and mind to attention and I am thankful. I know of your grace for I have been a recipient. I know of your peace for I have experienced healing. I know of your mercy for I have witnessed human change. City dwelling is harsh, loud, and unrelenting. Tall buildings obscure the rising and setting sun. The sights and sounds of nature are being obliterated. Your holy Presence is as soft as the whisper of a butterfly, and as gentle. You call me out of busyness to moments of quiet and repose, and I am being made stronger. Walk with me through the remaining hours of this day. In the power of Christ Jesus, I pray. Amen.

Evening

Great living Redeemer, continue to bless and watch over me even when I flee from your side. Prepare my heart, O God, for the coming of your Holy Spirit. Work in me a spirit of newness; enable me to receive, as if the first hearing the glad-joyous message that Christ is alive and will find me. Help me to live with the implications of that reality. Empower me to orient my life around that central truth. May it be my anchor and the source of daily strength. Teach me more of the art of healing, and may my life reveal the living Christ at work within me. Amen.

Scripture

You are the salt of the earth; but if salt has lost its taste, how can its saltiness be restored? It is no longer good for anything, but is thrown out and trampled under foot. You are the light of the world. A city built on a hill cannot be hid. No one after lighting a lamp puts it under the bushel basket, but on the lampstand, and it gives light to all in the house. In the same way, let your light shine before others, so that they may see your good works and give glory to your Father in heaven.

Matthew 5:13–16

You are the light of the world. A city built on a hill cannot be hid.

Matthew 5:14

Day 23

Morning

Mighty Creator and ever-creating God, with the breaking of dawn of each new day you renew my spirit and my energies. You give me new life, and invite me into faithfulness. Take my mind, heart, body, and soul and use all of me in the living of your Gospel. Lead me into deeper levels of holiness. Help me this day to see new ways of sharing your Gospel with those who are most in need. Help me to see and live beyond the immediate and to orient all of my life in the light of eternity. This day, bless my living with wholeness, and grant me the grace of being a blessing. By the Sacred Life of Christ, I pray. Amen.

Midday

Wonderful, mighty, ever-present God, it is in your holy Presence that we discern fullness of health: strength of body, clarity of mind, and richness of soul. At noon I pause for refreshment and rest for my body. For my mind I seek focus, clarity of intention, and new creative thought. In these brief moments of communion with you, deepen me down until I see with unclouded vision the depths of my eternal soul, and thus strengthen me to live in fullness for you. On these city streets, in hospitals, in places of pain, bereavement, and brokenness, I pray that I may travel with Christ, in whose Name I pray. Amen.

Evening

God of all power, mercy, and intimacy, you invite me to look within my innermost self; to be quiet, to listen to the silence, to wait and discern your intimate Presence, your loving care, your peace, and your will for me. Help me to pause and to reconstruct the blessings that I have received this day, and, by the recounting, to retain them in my memory bank of thanksgiving. For my past redemption, for my present liberation, and for my sanctification which is still in process, I bow in humility and with a thankful heart. Bless my dreams with material worthy of your Presence, and throughout the night grant me restorative sleep. I pray in the Name of Christ Jesus, my Savior, and Spiritual Friend. Amen.

Scripture

At that time the disciples came to Jesus and asked, "Who is the greatest in the kingdom of heaven?" He called a child, whom he put among them, and said, "Truly I tell you, unless you change and become like children, you will never enter the kingdom of heaven. Whoever becomes humble like this child is the greatest in the kingdom of heaven. Whoever welcomes one such child in my name welcomes me. If any of you put a stumbling block before one of these little ones who believe in me, it would be better for you if a great millstone were fastened around your neck and you were drowned in the depth of the sea."

Matthew 18:1–6

Whoever welcomes one such child in my name welcomes me.

Matthew 18:5

Day 24

Morning

Nourishing-sustaining-caring God, you invite me to be a Disciple and to follow in your path. You travel at a pace that always has you out in front, and, when I fall behind and lose sight, your voice beckons me to catch up. When I become distracted by the attractions along the way, you call out to me and remind me of your nearness. In your Presence I become recollected and made whole. I become reoriented and gain strength for the continuation of the journey. Daily you strengthen my faith; you renew my energies; you restore my soul again, and again, and again. I kneel beside Peter, James, Thomas, and Mary Magdalene, and pray to Jesus, my Redeemer and Soul Friend. Amen.

Midday

Mightily intimate God of health and strength, you see all and know all. Before the dawn of creation you were. While we were being formed in our mothers' wombs you were there. In all of our past comings and goings you were there. In all of this day's activities you are present. Great Master Teacher, enable me to see, to feel, and to know your abiding Presence. Like under the mighty, caring wing of a mother eagle, keep me close under your protecting care. In and through the plain and ordinary events of my living, teach me more of your Holy mysteries. Great Divine Master, in your Presence I kneel as a blind beggar in order that I may stand upright and see clearly. Help me to provide healing and hope in the minute particulars. With the power of Christ alive within me, I pray. Amen.

Evening

Holy Jesus, Wholly God, great Divine Liberator, during the daylight hours there were moments of grace that interrupted and blessed the common and the routine. Those surprise gifts of grace awakened me out of dullness, and strengthened my mind and soul. At the close of day I pause to remember, and to recount the surprise visits of divine grace. Help me to live a life of thanksgiving. You claim me as your own and invite me to live as a Follower. Watch over me during each of the watches of the night, and wake me with the dawn of a new day, refreshed and energized. Amen.

Scripture

Have you not known? Have you not heard? The LORD is the everlasting God, the Creator of the ends of the earth. He does not faint or grow weary; his understanding is unsearchable. He gives power to the faint, and strengthens the powerless. Even youths will faint and be weary, and the young will fall exhausted; but those who wait for the LORD shall renew their strength, they shall mount up with wings like eagles, they shall run and not be weary, they shall walk and not faint.

Isaiah 40:28–31

...but those who wait for the LORD shall renew their strength....

Isaiah 40:31

Day 25

Morning

Amazing-wonderful God of all majesty, miracles, and surprise visits, while I slept through the watches of night you watched over me and kept me safe from harm's way. With the breaking light and sounds of dawn, you awakened and stayed by my side until I was fully awake and conscious of being alive. Now during these early hours you gift me with the freedom of choice. You invite, welcome, and encourage me to choose divine companionship. Help me to be intentional with my usage of each passing hour and forgive me when I am not. Keep me free, safe, and whole on each of the paths that I walk, and when day is over call me again to prayer. Amen.

Midday

Deep and most Intimate God, you are beyond gender, class, and color. You are more than all holiness. You evade all capture and any control. You are beyond all language. We know you only by metaphor, yet all metaphors are inadequate. Most Holy God, you are always accessible and continually nurturing. You offer yourself freely to us, your human creatures. You rescue. You invite. You encourage. With the falling of the first snow of winter, we are reminded that, separated from your Holy warmth, our hearts are cold. Surround our wintered lives with your love. In the Holiness of Jesus, I pray. Amen.

Evening

Almighty, merciful, and most intimate God, you relate to me as one who loves, watches over, and cares for me in all my needs and desires. You, O Holy One, prompt me daily to live and envisage that which you created me to be. Teach me more about prayer. Teach me how to be quiet. May the power of holy listening bear fruit in me daily. Strengthen both my body and mind. Bless my soul with integrity and purity of desire. Use all of me for your purposes. Grant me rest, peace, and holy dreams while I sleep. In the Name of Christ, I pray. Amen.

Scripture

He said to them, "Come away to a deserted place all by yourselves and rest a while." For many were coming and going, and they had no leisure even to eat. And they went away in the boat to a deserted place by themselves. Now many saw them going and recognized them, and they hurried there on foot from all the towns and arrived ahead of them. As he went ashore, he saw a great crowd; and he had compassion for them, because they were like sheep without a shepherd; and he began to teach them many things.

Mark 6:31–34

He said to them, "Come away to a deserted place all by yourselves and rest a while."

Mark 6:31

Day 26

Morning

Eternal and most intimate God, your years are from everlasting to everlasting. Wonderful and amazing God, you transcend space and time and yet involve yourself in every present moment. Like a loving grandparent who lifts a beloved toddler onto a lap and there cradles her, so this day draw me closer into the realm of your Holiness. Great, caring, and inviting God, this day stir in my heart, my mind, and my soul. Help me to lift up my eyes and my spirit to see the distant vistas of your vision of humanity. Stir my sleeping courage and awaken my slumbering resolve to involve myself in the labors of your Holy realm that is "ever coming" and "already arrived." I would stand this day by the side of Jesus on the Mountain of Temptation, and pray. Amen.

Midday

Gracious, generous, and joyous God, you know both labor and rest. Help me in the remaining hours of this day to add such dimensions to my life. I am conscious of my use of time and strive to be a good steward of it. But, generous God, in my preoccupation with doing and getting more done, oftentimes I am an unwise steward with time. Help me to place aside every anxiety about doing. Keep me conscious of my usage of the gift of time. Liberate me from the need and desire of "doing more." May there be a preponderance of joy in the manner of my labor. And when this day is over, grant me rest. Amen.

Evening

ay is over and night has long since come. I am a weary traveler, I need rest, and I seek your benediction on this day. As I review my activities, thoughts, and deeds, I place all of them in your grace-filled care. My life has been enriched by the men and women who passed my way and with whom I shared companionship. Great Master Teacher of all mysteries, infuse my life with the learnings of this day and make them permanent. I pray that I may have restorative rest and peaceful sleep during each remaining hour of this night. These things I ask that I may be strengthened for another day. Amen.

Scripture

He came out and went, as was his custom, to the Mount of Olives; and the disciples followed him. When he reached the place, he said to them, "Pray that you may not come into the time of trial." Then he withdrew from them about a stone's throw, knelt down, and prayed, "Father, if you are willing, remove this cup from me; yet, not my will but yours be done." Then an angel from heaven appeared to him and gave him strength. In his anguish he prayed more earnestly, and his sweat became like great drops of blood falling down on the ground. When he got up from prayer, he came to the disciples and found them sleeping because of grief, and he said to them, "Why are you sleeping? Get up and pray that you may not come into the time of trial."

Luke 22:39–46

Then an angel from heaven appeared to him and gave him strength.

Luke 22:43

Day 27

Morning

Let not the freezing rain of winter, nor the scorching humid heat of summer detour my thoughts of you, great lover of my soul. At the beginning of this new day, surround my life with your all-encompassing Holy care, that I may gain focus and intentionality to my living. I pray that I may achieve joy and peace in my living this day; and I may exhibit hospitality and welcome to each that I encounter. May the crucified Christ remove all blinders and any slothfulness, stand me on my feet, and send me forth for the work of this day. I kneel by the side of my sisters, Martha and Mary, as I start this day. Amen.

Midday

Great spiritual companion of ultimates and intimates, the noontime whistles, bells, and sirens have long since sounded; I have completed a significant amount of work, some of which was quite good. Help me, in this present moment to pause, and to give thanks for the morning hours and my use of them. In these brief moments of quiet and silence, help me to regain the intentions and the orientation with which I began this day. For gifts this day received and discerned, gifts of the heart and mind; help me to be a faithful and wise steward. I kneel with and by my faith community and pray. Amen.

Evening

God of rest, night has come and the labors of the day have ceased. I now leave to your immediate and eternal judgment my use of your gift of this day. Where I have done less than I could, and when and where I erred in doing, let my soul confront and there forgive. For those experiences and friendships of this day that facilitated joy and nourished my soul, I am thankful. I recall and name them one by one and I am strengthened. Teach me how to be more quickly thankful for the little gifts of life. Now as I lie down to sleep, I pray that my body and mind will be strengthened by restful sleep. In the Holy Name of Christ Jesus, I pray. Amen.

Scripture

It was now about noon, and darkness came over the whole land until three in the afternoon, while the sun's light failed; and the curtain of the temple was torn in two. Then Jesus, crying with a loud voice, said, "Father, into your hands I commend my spirit." Having said this, he breathed his last. When the centurion saw what had taken place, he praised God and said, "Certainly this man was innocent." And when all the crowds who had gathered there for this spectacle saw what had taken place, they returned home, beating their breasts. But all his acquaintances, including the women who had followed him from Galilee, stood at a distance, watching these things.

Luke 23:44–49

"Father, into your hands I commend my spirit."

Luke 23:46

Day 28

Morning

Great and magnificent God, I struggle to name you "who are more than" and "closer by" anything that I can conceive of when sounding the name God. Deepest and most intimate, holy mystery, dwell with me this day, that all that I am, and all that I aspire to be and do, will bear the mark of wholeness. In your holy Presence may I see with fresh eyes the brokenness and pain of this world. Enable me to look into the depths of my own soul and there to be strengthened. With your gift of this new day to me, may I be a healer at the depths of individual brokenness. May I bring realizable hope to the corporate structures and systems that are at times the source of pain and misery. With James and Paul in Jerusalem, I kneel to pray. Amen.

Midday

Great God of mystery, intimacy, health and wholeness, during the morning hours, in the midst of work, I have known your Presence, and experienced your grace. Now at midday I pause to reflect on the morning hours and to refocus my intentions and my energies for the remaining hours of this day. Help me to see each segment of time as potentially full of meaning. Teach me to be fully alive in every present moment. Help me not to misuse, abuse, or waste any of the precious moments of life. Teach me to be more quickly thankful and more ready to believe in the goodness of God. With the young lad with five barley loaves and two fish, who offered all, I pray. Amen.

Evening

Wonderful-mighty God of grace and peace, the evening shadows have fallen on another day. I know that there is no health or wholeness to be found in rushing and busyness, but I confess, I have this day enjoyed the frenzied pace of doing, and doing, and doing. God of all spiritual reality and medical truth, deliver me this hour from the speed demon. Set me free for time in contemplation every day. Enable me to place meditation in front of work. Great caring God, protect and guard both my heart and soul, even when I do not. Through each hour of the night grant me rest and sleep. I kneel by the side of Martha, my sister, and pray. Amen.

Scripture

I have said these things to you while I am still with you. But the Advocate, the Holy Spirit, whom the Father will send in my name, will teach you everything, and remind you of all that I have said to you. Peace I leave with you; my peace I give to you. I do not give to you as the world gives. Do not let your hearts be troubled, and do not let them be afraid. You heard me say to you, "I am going away, and I am coming to you." If you loved me, you would rejoice that I am going to the Father, because the Father is greater than I.

John 14:25–28

"Peace I leave with you; my peace I give to you."

John 14:27

Day 29

Morning

Wonderful and magnificent Creator God, ever-present and still creating, you are for me faithful friend and spiritual companion through the heights and depths and all the "in betweens" of my daily life. You invite and encourage me to establish a dwelling place within the realms of holiness. Before I begin the labors of this day, help to focus my intentions, my energies, my time, and my thoughts on the life of faith and caring. For the labors of this day that await, strengthen my body, mind, and soul for faithful stewardship in life that Christ Jesus gives. Amen.

Midday

Glorious God of grace and power, the morning hours have been busy and productive, now I pause to acknowledge and to render thanks for your watchful care. Your abiding Presence is truly amazing. Let me never take for granted or depart from your whole-making Presence. Continue to surround my life. Help me to see where I am blind. Cleanse from my eyes the glitter of a culture which exercises a heavy influence on my life and faith. Help me to see and to think more clearly. May the power of the Holy Spirit surround, purify, and energize every dimension of my life. I stand in awe, with Peter, James, and John on the Mount of Transfiguration, and pray. Amen.

Evening

Amazing, wonderful God of grace and mercy, my labors this day have not been without flaw. Desiring to be and do more, I did less than I could have. I was seldom focused or clear with my intentions. I drifted and wasted time. My life energy was scattered aimlessly. I was ill-tempered and short on patience. Those who saw me this day would scarcely know the One to whom I have pledged faithfulness. Merciful God, forgive my offenses and my sloth. Now at this late evening hour grant me sleep and restorative rest. Wake me with the fresh promise of a new day restored and invigorated. Within the loving, healing arms of Christ, I pray. Amen.

Scripture

But now I am coming to you, and I speak these things in the world so that they may have my joy made complete in themselves. I have given them your word, and the world has hated them because they do not belong to the world, just as I do not belong to the world. I am not asking you to take them out of the world, but I ask you to protect them from the evil one. They do not belong to the world, just as I do not belong to the world. Sanctify them in the truth; your word is truth. As you have sent me into the world, so I have sent them into the world. And for their sakes I sanctify myself, so that they also may be sanctified in truth.

John 17:13–19

"But now I am coming to you, and I speak these things in the world so that they may have my joy made complete in themselves."

John 17:13

Day 30

Morning

Wonderful, personal, most intimate God of nurture, strength and encouragement, at this early morning hour I pause to seek your blessing on this day. Enable me to clarify my intentions about my use of the hours of the day. Unite my prayers with the manner in which I live. May there be around me and within me an awareness of the Holy Spirit that seeks to bless and empower. Through each hour of this day strengthen me—heart, mind, body, and soul. May the manner of my living be strength for self and others. Teach me to more quickly recognize your Presence in the midst of the ordinary events, and there respond. With head bowed and knees bent, I am the one in need of prayer. Amen.

Midday

Merciful God of blessings: blessings of the past, blessings of the present, and blessings yet to be received, help me to make the daily counting of my blessings a regular routine. Enable me to seek sufficient quantities of silence until I am blessed by the memory of all your blessings. Keep me silent until I recall all blessings: blessings forgotten and blessings given but not discerned. Keep me silent until I am blessed with a holy memory. Help me never to become so busy or preoccupied with work that I should ever forget the true nature of all work. At midday let me be refreshed, refocused, and energized. Great and magnificent God, truly you have given of yourself to me. I am both humbled and thankful. With all the saints, I pray. Amen.

Evening

Ever-creating and faithful God of day and night, of labor and of rest, this day I experienced the Presence of holiness in the lives of others, but knew it not until afterwards. I am humbled by those experiences where simple skills freely shared became a learning moment for another. Help me to be continually conscious of the teaching power contained in genuine human care. Help me to be ever alert to where, in the regular events of daily life, caring, sharing, and giving can become an extraordinary teaching moment. Great masterful Teacher, teach me more of the art of compassionate teaching. Amen.

Scripture

Who will separate us from the love of Christ? Will hardship, or distress, or persecution, or famine, or nakedness, or peril, or sword?

No, in all these things we are more than conquerors through him who loved us. For I am convinced that neither death, nor life, nor angels, nor rulers, nor things present, nor things to come, nor powers, nor height, nor depth, nor anything else in all creation, will be able to separate us from the love of God in Christ Jesus our Lord.

Romans 8:35; 37–39

... in all these things we are more than conquerors through him who loved us.

Romans 8:37

Day 31

Morning

Most holy and mighty God, your grace surrounds my life and blesses me day after day. Great lover of my soul, you have blessed and blessed and blessed my life repeatedly. Most intimate spiritual companion of my soul, you bestow on my life blessings that are unexpected and unannounced. Let me begin this new day by being quiet and listening to the holy whispers. Awaken in my memory banks past blessings received. May the power of memory enliven me for the labors of the day. Empower me to live this day with the certain knowledge that God is, that God watches over, and that God cares for me. By the side of the road to Jericho, as one in need, I pray. Amen.

Midday

Mighty God of liberating peace and redemptive love, the morning has been long, and much good and productive work has been completed. Your holy Presence was near. Help me to see the remaining hours of this workday as a sacred trust. Help me to be conscious of time and my use of it, but let me never become obsessed or paralyzed by segments of time that are unproductive. Let there be long moments of wonder. May I create space so that wise angels can visit my mind and my heart. Enable me this day to find the time to think and to feel. May there be some individual moments of time just for quiet and silence. Within the protective healing arms of Jesus I work and pray. Amen.

Evening

Mighty God of wisdom and loving care, you have blessed me with another day of life. I seemed to have done so little with all that was entrusted to my care. Help me to gather together the people with whom this day was shared. Let me name them one by one until all are remembered. May the activities of this day past add new understanding to my faith. May the memories of this day enliven my aims and deeds for tomorrow. May my heart be always pure. May my mind be clear and focused. May my intentions be honest. Now at the close of this day grant me rest and sleep. Protect me through the night and awaken me at the dawn of another new day. Amen.

Scripture

For I handed on to you as of first importance what I in turn had received: that Christ died for our sins in accordance with the scriptures, and that he was buried, and that he was raised on the third day in accordance with the scriptures, and that he appeared to Cephas, then to the twelve. Then he appeared to more than five hundred brothers and sisters at one time, most of whom are still alive, though some have died. Then he appeared to James, then to all the apostles. Last of all, as to one untimely born, he appeared also to me. For I am the least of the apostles, unfit to be called an apostle, because I persecuted the church of God.

I Corinthians 15:3–9

Last of all, as to one untimely born, he appeared also to me.

I Corinthians 15:8

Of Related Interest ...

Prayer When It's Hard to Pray

Martin C. Helldorfer

The author makes clear the point that people's lives—and, thus, their prayer lives—are an integration of high and low experiences, of times of feeling in sync with God and others, and times of feeling alone and out of touch. He offers ways to weather the storms that can disrupt anyone's prayer life.

ISBN: 0-89622-602-6, 80 pp, $7.95

Songs of Sunrise, Seeds of Prayer

Wayne Simsic

Through personal experiences of respecting, reverencing and experiencing nature, the author's life became a hymn of praise. He suggests that reverence for God's Creation can transform us into deeper union with God.

ISBN: 0-89622-600-X, 133 pp, $9.95

Psalms for Times of Trouble

John Carmody

The author is openly realistic in this book of prayers that were forged in the darkness and trouble of his own battle with terminal cancer. Yet the prayers hold out hope in the eternal kindness and mercy of God.

ISBN: 0-89622-614-X, 168 pp, $9.95

Good Morning, Lord

Everyday Prayers for Everyday People

Joseph T. Sullivan

Here are 365 brief, yet thoughtful prayers, one for each day of the year. They deal with ordinary events and feelings, as well as those arising from extraordinary situations.

ISBN: 0-89622-593-3, 200 pp, $9.95

Available at religious bookstores or from

XXIII TWENTY-THIRD PUBLICATIONS

P.O. Box 180 • Mystic, CT 06355 • 1-800-321-0411